Worthy

Amanda Germano

BookLeaf Publishing

India | USA | UK

Presentation by *BookLeaf Publishing*

Web: www.bookleafpub.com

E-mail: info@bookleafpub.com

ISBN: 9789358313598

First edition 2023

To my mama, who has always encouraged my love of writing. Thank you for being a constant cheerleader in my life. You always told me that writing is my gift. You believed in me long before I believed in myself. Thank you.

To my boys, Michael and Dominic, may you always pursue your dreams and do what brings you joy. Always know that you can do hard things. I will always be here to support, encourage and believe in you. I am so proud to me your mama. I love you forever.

ACKNOWLEDGEMENT

To my family, my parents and siblings. I'm grateful for you. You're at the foundation of who I am. You've seen all versions of me, and I know no matter where we're at or what we're doing in life, I can count on you.

To every person mentioned in these poems, and anyone who played a role in my life story- friend, family, stranger... thank you for the impact you've made. I honor you with these poems.

To my husband - thanks for supporting me throughout this journey and helping me find some time each day to write. It's been a blessing being able to carve out some personal time for me to reconnect with something I love doing.

And most importantly, I acknowledge the Lord, for blessing me with this passion for writing, for never abandoning or forsaking me, and for leading me out of deep waters.

PREFACE

For me, writing has always been a passion, a form of self-expression, a creative outlet and an emotional release. From keeping countless diaries and journals as a child, to joining writer's club in high school, to keeping an online blog for family and friends to document a post-collegiate volunteer year of service, it's always been a hobby of mine to write. Aside from a few published articles in various websites, I've never taken a step to have anything published. This feels like a dream come true, but at the same time, absolutely terrifying. But that's a step toward growth, right? Doing things that scare you. Facing your fears of unworthiness, not being good enough, or not having what it takes. I think there's power and freedom in that. I am excited to do some unpacking, processing and healing through this book. Thanks for coming along for the ride.

What is a Poem?

do poems have to rhyme?
do they have to make sense?
should they be inspiring?
or dive into the mess?

does the storyline matter?
or can it just flow?
can they be about anything?
or something I personally know?

What form is the best?
Limerick, sonnet, haiku?
Would you maybe be impressed
if they were all actually true?

So here's my attempt
my feeble attempt
to bring beauty from my mess

To unpack, and sort out and heal from
some things I have never addressed

So here we go, it's time to share
these poems that stem from my story

With faith and hope, it is my prayer
that God receives the glory.

Mirror

Mirror mirror on the wall
you're too short, you're too tall
you're too skinny, you're too fat
where'd you learn to dress like that?
your ears are too big
your eyes are too close
your chin is indented
gosh, look at that nose!
that pimple, that freckle,
that mole and that scar,
no one will ever love you
the way that you are.

Mirror's Response

Oh beautiful girl who is looking at me,
Oh, what a difference in what we both see

Unique and beloved and made with care
That's what I see, while deeply you stare
The way that you look, is but a small part
Of your value and beauty that stem from your
heart

Your face and your hair and your body is home
For your lively divine spirit to roam
You're learning and growing and changing each
day
But your value and worth won't ever go away

The way that you are, it's the perfect design
Your body, your soul, your heart and your mind
The same God who made the sun, moon and
stars
Put His paintbrush on you and loves you just as
you are.

Sandy

Just 14 years old, I'm the star of the show
Community theater, you've pushed me to grow
You've given me confidence, a love for myself
Helped me realize my talents, I'd kept up on a
shelf

I'm leading the cast, this is my time
With main character energy, I'm ready to shine
Look at me, I'm Sandra Dee
My heart, body and soul feels free

For years, I tucked away and hid
Afraid of my own shadow;
Self-conscious, shy and reserved, but now
A theater girl, ready to glow

On the stage is where I want to be
Not sitting in the crowd
I want to dance and act and sing
And live my passion and joy, out loud

This hobby and dream, it's been put on hold
Years have passed since I've been on a stage
I'll always be grateful for the opportunity
For my passion and talents to engage

Theater, my friend, you saved me, it's true
And helped me find out who I am
I'll be back, one day, though not right now
Until then, I love you and thank you.

Lisa

You drove my bus to school freshman year
Your message of death rings strong in my ear
We'd chat in the mornings, you were typically
kind
But that one thing you said, can't escape from
my mind

It was cold and dark, I remember that clearly
We somehow began to talk about family
"I'm one of seven" I said with a smile
Your response was tasteless, nasty and vile

"Your mom should have had an abortion!", you
said
Tell me then, Lisa, which of us should be dead?
Which brother or sister should have been
deprived
of the gift and the right of just being alive?

You said it so blunt, almost proudly, in fact
I was hurt and surprised and taken aback

I sat there in silence, unsure what to say
But I think of you Lisa, even to this day
Those words that caused my heart to shatter

Are reflective of you- and your soul for that
matter

I choose to follow Jesus and He tells us to pray
For those who hurt and wrong us, each and
every day

So here's my heartfelt prayer
I promise that it's true.
Today and every day,
I choose to forgive you.

Anxiety Sprint

fears
running marathons in my head
never tiring
never stopping
not even for water
never quitting
never giving up
never giving in
relentless
until they reach the finish line
collecting gold silver and bronze
medals
at my expense

Unsubscribe

oh girl,
if only you knew
your value is not
measured by
a scale
nor a number on a tag

that the number of
calories you consume
or the number of
calories you burn

doesn't even come close
to your measure of worth.

these "tips and tricks"
disguised as "healthy hacks"
are tools to torture you
make you obsess over
shrinking yourself
to match the magazine models

your body was never the issue.
time to cancel the subscription.

Unspeakable Things

Let's speak about the unspeakable things.

Anxiety, depression, sexual assault
Drugs, overdoses, drinking to a fault.
Violence, abuse, all the forms that it takes.
And all the hearts and lives that it breaks.

It makes you uncomfortable? Well I think that is
good.
I think that's the point; it does and it should.

Imagine living with maybe one, maybe all.
Imagine the judgment you face as you fall.

The condemnation, the critics, the views
What was it that happened, that drove them to
use?

What happened to you, to make you abuse?
Why live in darkness, is it something you
choose?

Just stop being sad, its a simple solution
Says no one who lives with the mental pollution

The dark and the haze and the poison, it stays
Drives people to places they can't get away

Learn to suffer in silence to protect others' peace
Is this why we lose so many to their beasts?

Perhaps if we learned to support and be there
Walk with and lift up and show up and care

Help carry their burdens, stand beside them and
fight
Lift them out of their darkness by just being a
light.

Just wait and see the difference it brings
When we show up and speak of the unspeakable
things.

I-90

A yell for help from the side of the road,
With no second thought, I hang up the phone.
A man in a panic, but he's not alone
The scene I encounter, brings a chill to my
bones.

A horror movie scene, but this is actually real
Who on earth, this precious life, could steal?
A few more pull over, as cars continue to pass
A blood-covered girl, perhaps breathing her last

With no clue what happened or what even to do
I fell to the ground and prayed over you
I sat there and witnessed you pass into Glory
Two strangers, but now, I'm a part of your story

It's nothing short of tragic how it came to an end
But please know, sweet girl, you were
surrounded by friends
There were people who cared, who ran to your
side
To help and to hold you close, as you died.

You're healed now in Heaven, for this I do pray
My hope is we can meet again, one glorious day.

Intermission

We're halfway through this.
Embrace the silence, just breathe.
The show must go on.

Dan

Things took a turn for the worse overnight
I'd better get up there fast.
My friend had suffered for years with this plight,
Would cancer take him at last?

I left work that moment and hopped in my car,
The tears didn't wait long to fall.
Please hold on, I'm not that far
Cried out to God and every saint on call.

Eleven years of friendship is no small thing.
This friend became more like a brother
We'd laugh and drink beer, eat pie and sing,
Shared stories and jokes with each other

I find the room and enter with care
His parents and brother and loved ones are there
There is sadness and mourning, oh how it's not
fair!
But also, the presence of God, filled the air.

We cried and prayed and sat with you
As your soul, to Heaven, took flight
My friend, you fought so long and hard
And put up one hell of a fight.

What an honor it was to sit in that room,
and see you one last time.
Words don't do justice to the hole that's left here,
But I've tried to explain with this rhyme.

So until we cross paths again, dear friend,
Keep watch over us while we wait.
Though things on this earth had to come to an
end,
Please meet me at the Heavenly gate.

Survivor

Stay quiet, we don't talk about these things
Expect that you will be blamed and told it was
your fault
X-rays show broken hearts, not broken
self-esteem
Understand that you won't be understood
Act like it was no big deal, it happens all the
time
Learn what you could and should have done to
prevent it

Advocate for yourself and others like you.
Speak up and speak out, loudly.
Stand up and seek justice.
Acknowledge each feeling, allowing it to usher
in healing.
Understand that what happened was never your
fault.
Live in the truth that you are worthy of safe,
beautiful, respectful love.
Trust that though this was part of your story,
your story isn't over yet.

Pandemic Wedding

the pandemic is surging
little baby within me is growing
postpone it, till when?
there's no way of knowing

nobody knows, so go on with the show
this is what we're supposed to do, right?
everything's cancelled, guests gotta go
but I guess it'll do, it's alright

fake nails from the drug store
rent-a- makeup artist online
hairdresser comes to the empty hotel
this wasn't the plan, but it's fine

everything is different
this wasn't the dream
I'm aching at all that was lost
no parties, no showers, no celebrations
but I guess that this is the cost

we want to be married, of course this is true
but this wasn't the dream for saying "I do"

a quick chat with my brother who's still
overseas,
a binder of letters that loved ones did send,
another brother with a camera snaps memories
with my mom, sisters, and best friend

I put on my dress, shoes, jewelry and veil
We head to the church down the street
A walk down the aisle , to an empty church
But a live-stream is on, so that's sweet

The wedding is lovely, for that I am grateful
It all worked out as it should
Family and friends cheered us on from outside
in the parking lot to do what they could

to celebrate and offer their love from afar,
with cheers, bubbles and beeping from their car

my heart was full, but it also was broken
a weird feeling to even explain
some words will just have to be left unspoken
of the joy and the love amidst the pain

of my pandemic wedding that came to be,
in that fateful May of 2020.

Cold Case

an unexpected letter arrives in the mail
regarding my 2016 case
do they know who he is? is he in jail?
my eyes widen and my heart starts to race

something that happened so long ago
was it now being brought to light?
I had tucked it away, moved on with my life
so much has happened since that awful night

forced to open a wound that I hoped had been
healed
a year of rehashing the story
a cold case cracked open, a DNA hit,
my truth was finally being revealed

I arrived at the court house
when it was finally time
to look him in the eyes
and describe the crime

a moment of healing
but also despair
as I recounted something so
evil and sick and unfair

I watched as they took him off to prison
out of ashes, my spirit had risen
the power is not his any longer
I walk in freedom, even stronger

Grandpa

A man of few words
With a heart full of love,
My grandpa, dear grandpa,
Now watches us from above

His eyes full of joy
We knew he was proud
He showed us by actions
Love doesn't have to be loud

A father's love so grand,
Healed wounds he never knew were there
A man always doing for others
With a helping hand to spare

You loved your sons, grandkids and wife
Of that we are confidently sure
You brought comfort, peace and warmth to our
life
With a gentle care, so pure

My boys, your great-grands, they know about
you
They know Who you're with and that Heaven is
true

I'll never forget when we had to part ways,
I'll love you and miss you all the rest of my
days.

A Letter to my Boys

My precious and sweet babies,
you are my pride and joy.
My greatest gift and blessing,
my perfect little boys.

You're the dream I've always dreamt,
my greatest wish and prayer.
You're a precious piece of evidence
of God's tender love and care.

To the boys who made me mama
and shook me to my core.
You've changed and rearranged me
from who I was before.

I'll love you till forever
I'll always stand by you
My heartbeats on the outside,
just know these words are true.

I'll teach you to be loving,
patient, gentle and kind.
To nurture your heart,
body, soul and mind.

Born just seventeen months apart,
I'm so glad you have eachother
What an honor and a privilege
to be chosen as your mother

And if you ever cannot see me
or hear me, while apart
Just close your eyes and know
that I am always in your heart.

Mama's Lullaby

mama mama loves you so
mama loves to watch you grow
mama loves the things you do
mama is so proud of you
mama mama loves you so
mama hopes you always know

Reclaiming the Vow

let's go dancing in the rain
let's go gaze up at the stars
let's dive into an ocean
let's find Jupiter and Mars

let's explore this world together
let's make memories, me and you
let's go hiking up the mountains
let's make all our dreams come true

let's tuck away our insecurites
let's grow from our mistakes
let's love and heal eachother
let's figure out what it takes

let's give it our best shot
let's remember who we are
let's forget who we are not

let's run from all the lies
let's cling to what is true
let's rely on faith and love
let's recommit to "I do"

A Poem For My Therapist

for letting me ramble
and seeing me cry
for helping me process
and figure out why

for a cup of warm tea
endless empathy
helping my sanity
for you I am thankful

for giving me tools
and challenging me
for holding me up
and endless honesty

for being a therapist but also a friend
for you I am thankful, forever amen

Applause

hey mama you did it
you did something new
you finally decided to
take time for you

look at you now
with your book that you wrote
possibilities are endless
now we'll end on this note

the moments of doubt
yes they crept in for sure
thinking you couldn't do it
though your intentions were pure

it's time to reclaim what you know to be true
you can do anything you put your mind to

End Scene

The show has ended
Time to take the final bow
Curtain close, thank you.